PLAY BY PLAY
SOCCER

Coach Lori Coleman and these Richfield athletes were photographed for this book:
   Rachael Ekholm,
   Mandy Engberg,
   Nate Evans-Winkel,
   Angelina Gearhart,
   Casey Herbert,
   Ernest Julean,
   Kacie Larson,
   Vas Leckas,
   Nichole Legus,
   Jennifer Lenberg,
   Neil Lenzen,
   Elizabeth Petrik,
   Marissa Santos,
   Niels Sorensen,
   Erick Stevens.

LERNER SPORTS
A DIVISION OF LERNER PUBLISHING GROUP

PLAY BY PLAY
SOCCER

Lori Coleman

Photographs by Andy King

Lerner Publications Company ● Minneapolis

Copyright © 2000 by Lerner Publications Company

All rights reserved. International copyright secured. No part of this book may be reproduced or transmitted in any form or by any means, electronic or mechanical, including photocopying and recording, or by any information storage or retrieval system, without permission in writing from Lerner Publications Company, except for the inclusion of brief quotations in an acknowledged review.

Library of Congress Cataloging-in-Publication Data
Coleman, Lori.
   Play by play. Soccer / Lori Coleman; photographs by Andy King.
     p. cm.
   Rev. ed. of: Fundamental soccer. ©1995
   Includes bibliographical references and index.
   Summary: Explores the history, skills and techniques of soccer.
   ISBN 0-8225-9876-0 (pbk. : alk. paper)
   1. Soccer—Juvenile literature. [1. Soccer.] I. Coleman, Lori. Fundamental soccer. II. King, Andy, ill. III. Title.
GV 943.25.C65 2000
796.334—dc21
                                      99-047670

Manufactured in the United States of America
1 2 3 4 5 6 – GPS – 05 04 03 02 01 00

Photo Acknowledgments
Photographs are reproduced with the permission of: pp. 7, 8 (both), The Bettman Archive; p. 9, ©ALL-SPORT USA/David Cannon; p. 27, ©Jon Van Woerden; p. 58, Mark Backlund/Courtesy of Corner Kick Indoor Soccer Center, Maplewood, Minn.

CONTENTS

Chapter 1 ....How This Game Got Started....................7
Chapter 2 ....Basics.. 11
Chapter 3 ....Game Time.. 33
Chapter 4 ....Practice, Practice............................... 43
Chapter 5 ....Razzle Dazzle..................................... 53
Soccer Talk.. 59
Further Reading.. 62
Index.. 63

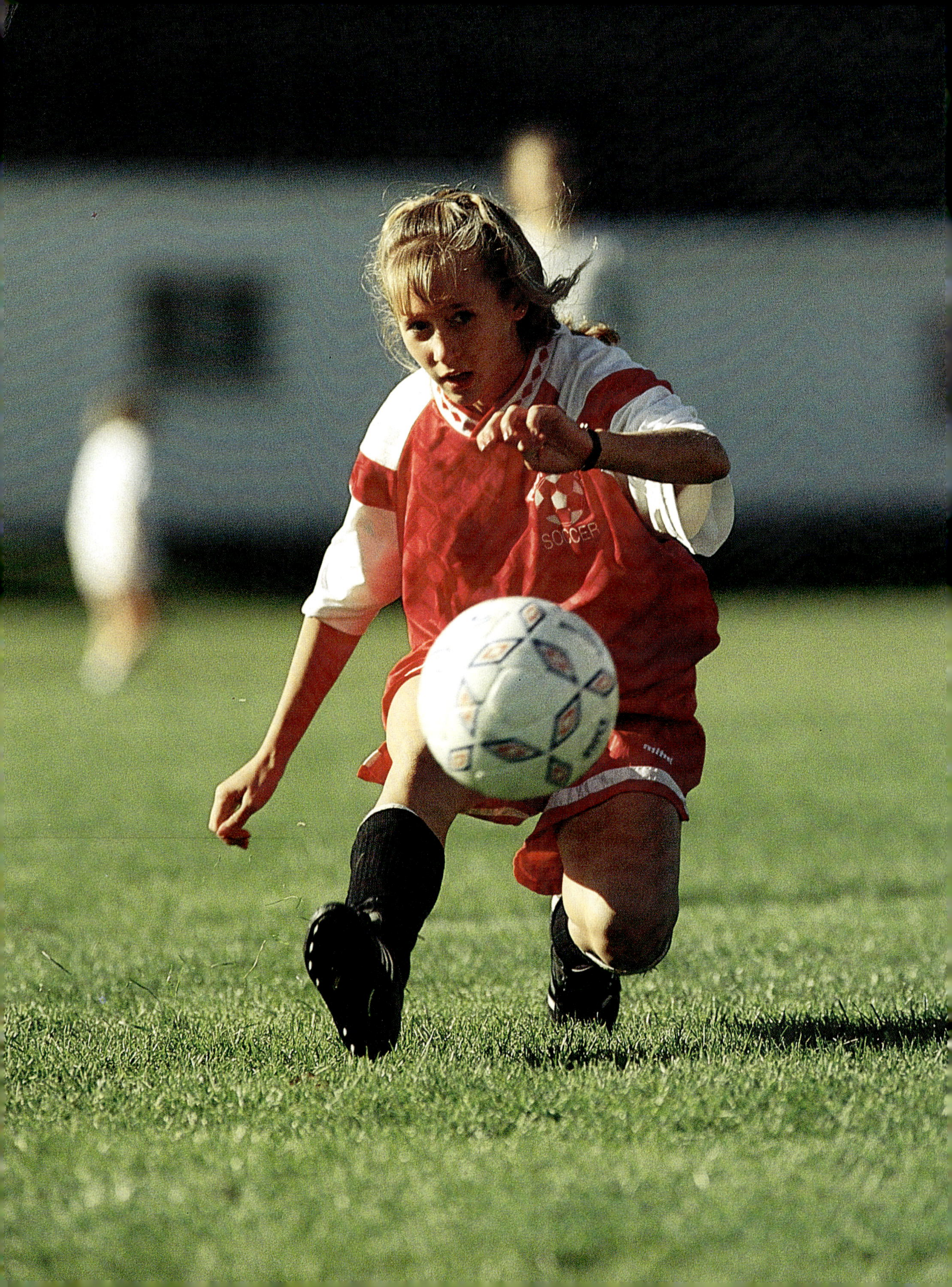
SOCCER

Chapter 1

HOW THIS GAME GOT STARTED

Soccer is a fast-moving game with lots of action. In a soccer game, two teams of 11 players move the ball around a large field with quick passes and hard kicks.

The only thing more exciting than watching a soccer game is playing the game yourself. More people play and watch soccer than any other team sport, including baseball, basketball, and hockey. In the United States alone, more than 18 million athletes play in youth soccer leagues. Soccer is the national sport of many countries in Europe, Asia, Africa, and South America.

Games like soccer have been played all over the world since ancient times. Most historians agree that a game very like modern soccer

This Greek sculpture from the fifth century shows a soccer player practicing his moves.

Early Romans played soccer.

was first played in Derby, England, around A.D. 217, when Romans occupied the country. In England, the game became known as football.

For centuries, soccer was popular even though a player could only use his or her feet, torso, or head to move the ball. Hands could not be used. Then in 1823, another game—later called rugby—was invented. Rugby players could use their hands to catch and throw the ball.

The London Football Association was formed in protest against the way rugby players carried the ball. Association members called the original version of football "association

This drawing shows an American soccer match in 1890.

football" to distinguish it from rugby. The name was shortened to "assoc" and later became "soccer," although the English and other Europeans continued to call it football.

Soccer was the only football game in the United States until the 1870s, when American football first became popular. In 1913, the United States Football Association was formed to govern the sport of soccer. In 1945, the governing body became known as the United States Soccer Federation (USSF).

The USSF runs professional, amateur, and youth soccer programs. The USSF organizes and manages national teams that play teams from other countries. The American Youth Soccer Organization (AYSO) organizes many leagues and tournaments for players under 18 years of age.

The Federation Internationale de Football Association (FIFA) governs soccer at the international level. More than 158 nations belong to FIFA. Most soccer games are played by FIFA rules.

FIFA holds a very popular tournament, called the World Cup, every four years. All member nations can compete to become one of the top 32 teams that play in the tournament.

The men's World Cup games were held in the United States in 1994. The Brazilian men won the final. In 1998, the French team won the cup.

In the 1990 World Cup Final, West Germany delighted its fans by defeating Argentina 1–0.

In 1999, the women's World Cup was held in the United States. More than 90,000 people crammed into the Rose Bowl in Pasadena, California, for the final between the United States and China.

The American women thrilled their fans by winning the championship in a shootout with China. After the game ended in a scoreless tie, the two teams played two overtime periods before going to the shootout. Five members of each team took a shot on goal. U.S. goalkeeper Briana Scurry made the only save, and the United States won, 5-4.

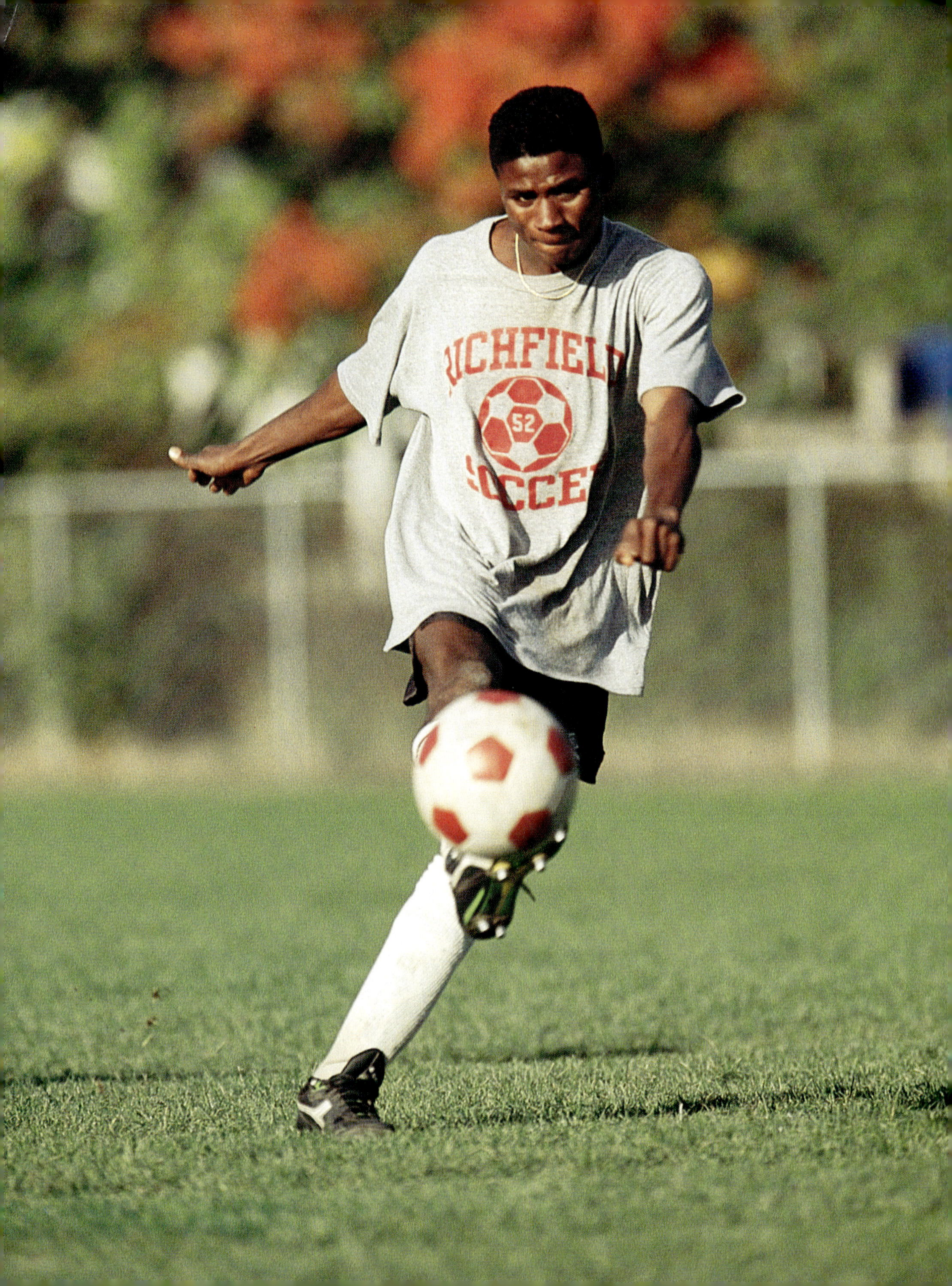
52

Chapter 2

BASICS

A soccer field is always a large rectangle, but it can be from 100 to 130 yards long and from 50 to 100 yards wide. A **center line** divides the field in half, and a **center spot** directly in the middle of the field is encircled by the **center circle.** The ball is put in play at the center spot, to start a game.

A **goal** 8 yards wide and 8 feet high stands at each end of the field. Netting is stretched between two **goalposts** on the sides and a **crossbar** across the top. When a player is able to kick the ball into the opponent's goal, the player's team scores a point.

Around the **goal area** is a larger **penalty area,** which extends 18 yards out from the goal. The **penalty spot** lies within the penalty area. The **corner areas** and **penalty arcs** are used when a rule has been broken.

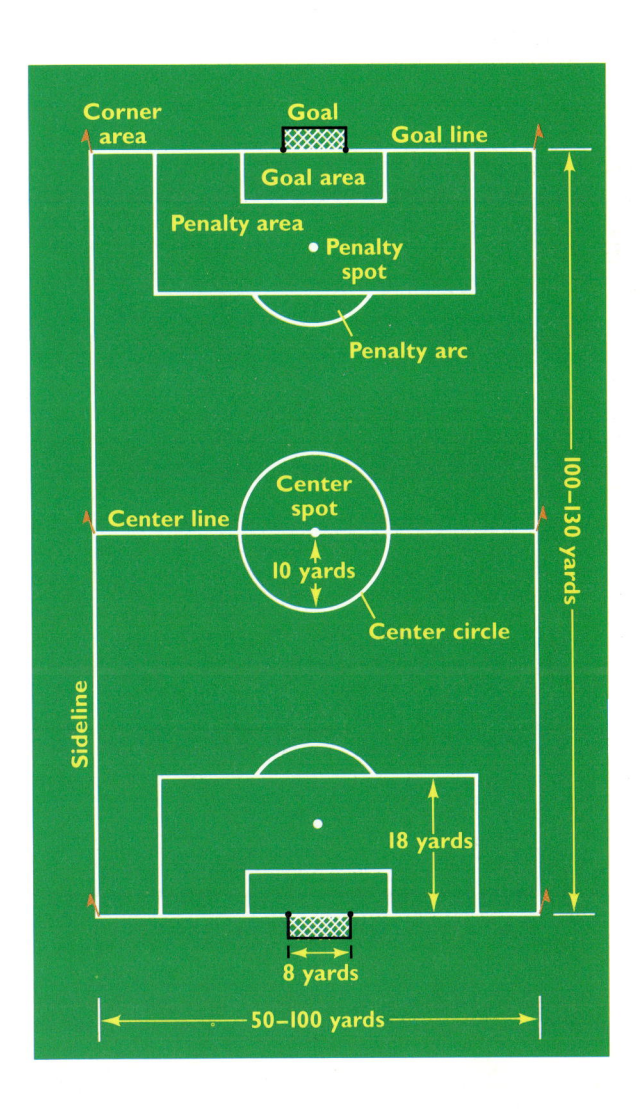

11

EQUIPMENT

Soccer shoes must fit correctly. Shoes that fit poorly can affect a player's performance and can even cause injury. Soccer shoes worn for regular outdoor play have rubber or plastic cleats. The cleats dig into the ground.

Most soccer players wear T-shirts and shorts while practicing. Jerseys, shorts, and long socks are the uniform for during a game. Players also wear shin guards and mouth guards to prevent injuries.

The **goalkeeper,** or goalie, wears a slightly different uniform from the other players on the team. The goalie wears gloves and a uniform with extra padding. The goalie's uniform must be a different color than that of his or her teammates' uniforms so that opponents can easily tell which player is the one allowed to use his or her hands.

BALLS

Soccer balls come in many colors and designs. The price of a ball depends on the brand, the material used, and the quality of its workmanship. Hand-sewn leather balls are softer and last longer than balls made from rubber or nylon, but synthetic balls are cheaper. An official soccer ball is 27 to 28 inches around and 14 to 16 ounces in weight.

BASIC MOVES

Soccer players move the ball on the field by running while controlling the ball with their feet. This move is called **dribbling.**

In the photographs below, Kacie is dribbling. With each step, she touches the ball with either the laces or outside of her foot. She uses both her left foot and her right foot while dribbling. After she is comfortable touching the ball with either foot, she practices dribbling while she is changing speeds, sprinting, and changing directions.

Being able to change speeds and directions while dribbling helps you maintain possession of the ball during a game.

One good way to get away from an opponent challenging you for the ball is to use a fake. Nate demonstrates how to do a fake in the photographs on this page.

With the ball close to him, Nate keeps his body between his opponent and the ball. To get away from the other player, he lunges one direction so that his opponent also moves that way. Then he touches the ball with the bottom of his foot, rolling it in the opposite direction. He quickly takes off dribbling in the opposite direction of his fake.

Passing is the quickest and surest way to move the ball. Accurate passes on the field are important for good teamwork.

First, practice passing with the inside of your foot. This is the safest pass because it is very accurate when done correctly. Place your nonkicking foot next to the ball. Hold the ankle of your kicking foot firmly for a crisp pass. After you hit the ball, follow through with your leg to give the pass more power.

Then, pass with the outside of your foot. This time, put your nonkicking foot far enough from the ball to give your kicking foot room to swing. Make sure you keep your ankle firm and follow through.

Finally, practice passing the ball long distances. For a more powerful kick that will send the ball a longer distance, pass with your **instep.** Hit the ball solidly with the laces of your shoe.

Inside of foot

Outside of foot

Instep of foot

On this page, Rachael demonstrates the **heel pass.** She places her non-kicking foot next to the ball. She swings back her kicking foot and hits the ball with her heel, sending a quick pass to a teammate behind her.

Sometimes there isn't time to stop the ball before passing it. To receive a ball and pass it all in the same motion, use the **one-touch pass.**

Position yourself directly in the ball's path. Swing your kicking foot as the ball reaches you, hitting it in the direction you want it to go.

17

If the ball is in the air, the one-touch pass is called a **volley pass.** Here, Rachael is in the ball's path and swings her leg to hit the ball with her foot.

Trapping is a skill that goes with passing. To receive a pass, you will often need to trap the ball and control it before you can continue play. Trapping is the way you stop the ball with your body and then put the ball in position to pass or dribble it.

You can trap a ball with your foot, thigh, abdomen, or chest. To trap a ground ball, lift your foot and tap the ball with the inside of your foot. Let your leg move back a little bit to soften the impact.

When the ball is bouncing or traveling in the air just over the ground, you can trap it with your instep. Hold your foot out, with the ankle firm, and trap the ball on the laces of your shoe.

When the ball is in the air, position yourself where the ball will land. Before it bounces on the ground, meet it with your thigh and draw back your leg when the ball hits.

Above, Kacie is trapping a high ball. She jumps to meet it with her abdomen. As the ball hits her, she keeps it under control by leaning into the ball with her body.

To trap even higher balls, players use their chest. In the photograph to the right, Kristy is using a chest trap. She controls where the ball will fall by turning her body when the ball hits her chest.

As the ball reaches her, Kristy gets in front of it and uses her upper chest as a table for the ball to land on. As the ball hits her, she leans her body forward and to the left so that the ball falls in that direction.

Shooting, like passing, requires accuracy. Shooting also calls for a very powerful kick. Use your instep to give your kick the most power. Mandy demonstrates how to shoot on this page and the next.

After she runs to the ball, Mandy places her nonkicking foot next to it and strikes the ball with the laces of her kicking foot. Mandy concentrates on keeping her ankle rigid. She follows through with her swinging leg.

Like passing, shooting can be done using either foot. You can also shoot with the outside of your foot. Still, most soccer players prefer to shoot with the instep of their strongest leg. Whatever shot you use, practice it often and you will score often.

Some players have trouble getting their foot underneath the ball to lift it into the air. Concentrate on hitting the ball with the correct part of your foot and then following through.

21

On this page, Casey is also trying to score goals, but instead of shooting, she is **heading** the ball. Heading means to hit the ball with your head at the hairline. Soccer players can use headers to send the ball downfield, to pass, or to score.

To head the ball, Casey watches the ball and positions herself where it will land. With her arms out in front of her, Casey moves to the ball.

Upon impact, she brings her shoulders forward, swings her arms back, keeps her neck and chin firm, and keeps her eyes open. Casey contacts the ball with her upper forehead, right at her hairline.

Be confident when you head the ball. Headers don't hurt when they are done correctly. Remember, you are hitting the ball instead of letting the ball hit you.

DEFENSE

When your team doesn't have the ball, you and your teammates play defense. All the players on a team must help with its defense for a team to succeed. **Marking** and **tackling** are important defensive skills.

To mark an opponent, stay close to the player while staying between that player and your team's goal.

If the player that you are marking has the ball, try to force that player to take the ball where you want it to go. For example, if you don't want the player to take a shot at the goal, force the opponent to the sideline and out of bounds.

You also must be able to tackle, or take the ball out of an opponent's control, when you are on defense.

While you are marking a player on the opposing team, try to force that player to stop and make a turn. Then, make your move to take away the ball and gain possession.

GOALKEEPING

The goalkeeper is the only player on the field who is allowed to use his or her hands to play the ball (except when a player is throwing in the ball from the sidelines).

In the photo at right, Elizabeth illustrates the **basic stance.** From the basic stance, the goalkeeper can reach, leap, and dive quickly. With her knees slightly bent, Elizabeth stands with her feet about shoulder-width apart. Her arms are raised and ready to stop any **shot on goal.** Shots that would go in the goal if the goalie didn't intercept them are called shots on goal.

Goalkeepers use positioning to minimize the goal area open to the opposing shooter. By moving off the goal line into the field, the goalkeeper makes the open goal space look smaller to the shooter. The goalie then can judge more easily where the shot will be aimed and block it.

Goalkeepers have to **collect,** or save, many shots on goal—rolling balls, bouncing balls, and high balls.

In the photos on this page, Nichole shows how to pick up rolling balls. She keeps her feet close enough together that the ball can't fit through them. Leaning over, she holds her hands out and slightly apart with the palms up. As she picks up the ball, she scoops it up to her chest.

KEEPER ! ! !

Tony Meola is one of the best goalkeepers born in the United States. Meola grew up in Kearny, New Jersey. He and his friends grew up watching the New York Cosmos, a professional team in the now-defunct North American Soccer League.

Meola grew up playing baseball as well as soccer. In high school, he was an all-state baseball player and an all-state soccer player. He had an opportunity to continue on in either sport, but Meola chose soccer. He played for the University of Virginia. Later he played for the U.S. team in the 1994 World Cup.

Meola, whose teammates call him "Meat" or "Meatball," is known as a tough keeper. He controls situations and affects plays before his opponents know what is happening. Meola often comes off the line and destroys an attack by intercepting a pass or stealing the ball from a dribbler. He can beat almost anyone in the air, and he can punt the ball more than 80 yards downfield.

To catch a ball in the air, Elizabeth positions herself so that her body is between the shot and the goal. She holds her hands with the palms out and her thumbs together so that her hands form a W.

To save high balls, the goalie must jump to reach them. Elizabeth sees a shot headed for the upper right corner of the goal. She gets into position and leaps on one leg, bringing the other knee up as she extends her arms to catch the ball in midair.

Sometimes the goalkeeper will not be able to reach a fast-moving shot quickly enough to catch the ball. In order to make a save, the goalkeeper may have to deflect the ball up over the goal or off to one side.

In the photograph at left, Nichole punches the ball over the goal. With her wrist and hand held firmly, she jumps up on one leg and punches the ball up and over the net with a short, quick stroke. She makes sure that the ball clears the goal.

Diving saves take a lot of work. Many goalies practice by diving from a kneeling position, as Rachael is. She kneels while a teammate tosses the ball to each side. As the ball nears, Rachael keeps her lower hand directly in the line of the ball's flight.

On this page, Elizabeth demonstrates how to make a diving save from the basic stance position.

As Elizabeth takes off from the basic stance, she extends her arms. When the ball hits her, she gathers it in and gets ready to hit the ground.

To soften her fall, Elizabeth rolls as she falls to the ground. She immediately gets up to see where her teammates are before she returns the ball to the playing field. Once the goalkeeper has made a save, he or she must put the ball back into play.

To pass the ball to a teammate nearby, the goalie throws the ball. To send the ball a longer distance, the goalkeeper **punts.**

The best punts are hard kicks that send the ball flying far but low to the ground. Before punting, take a couple of steps to build up your momentum. Hold the ball over your kicking foot, and swing your leg. For maximum distance, kick through the ball.

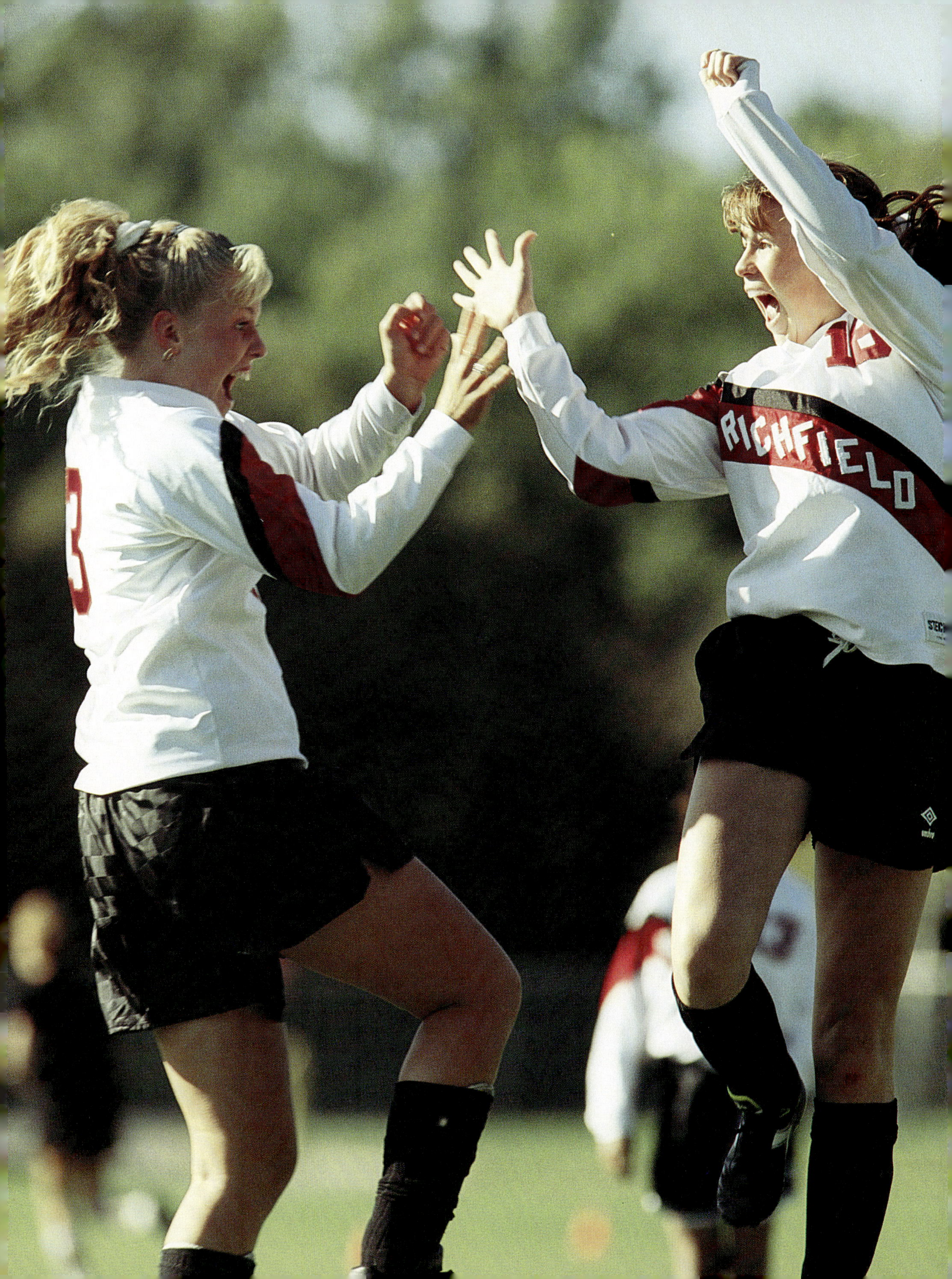
RICHFIELD

Chapter 3

GAME TIME

There are 11 players on a soccer team: one goalkeeper and 10 players in one of three basic positions: forward, fullback, and midfield.

Forwards pass the ball, support teammates with the ball, and dribble past defenders to get into a position where they can shoot. Forwards playing near the sidelines are **wings**.

Fullbacks mark opponents, try to force them to make a bad pass or dribble, and keep them out of the area in front of the goal. They cover for each other when one gets pulled out of position by the opponent he or she is marking.

Midfielders play both offense and defense. They help the forwards bring the ball down the field and into scoring position. They also help the fullbacks defend the goal.

4–3–3 Formation

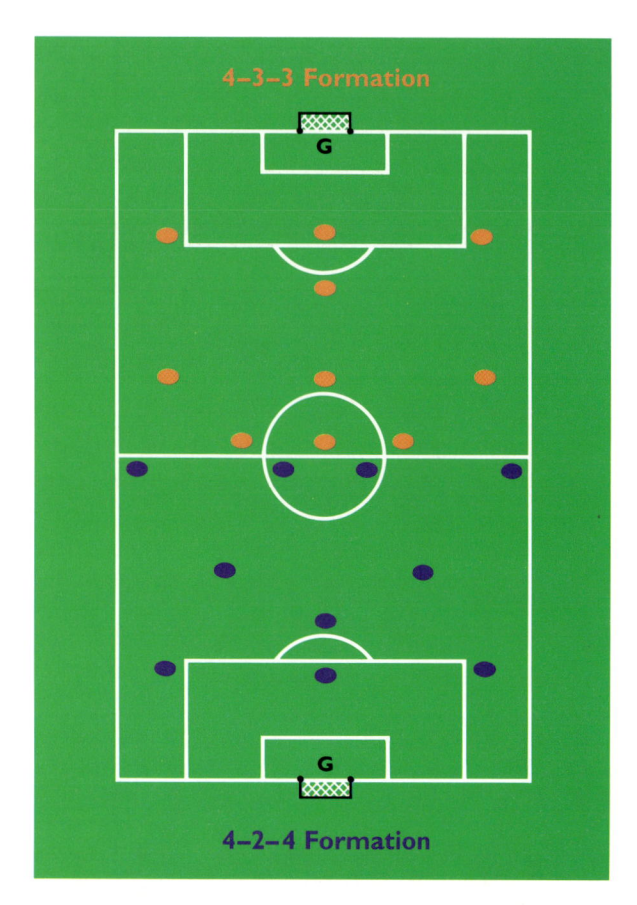

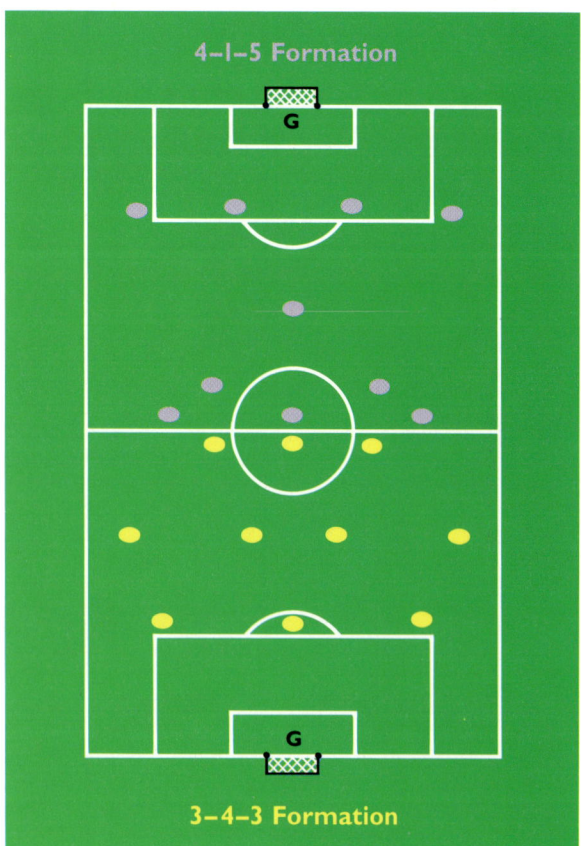

4–2–4 Formation

4–1–5 Formation

3–4–3 Formation

Some common formations of forwards, midfielders, and defenders are shown to the left.

RULES

A goal is scored when the entire ball crosses the goal line between the goalposts and under the crossbar. Each goal scored is one point. Ties are broken either by overtime periods or by shootouts.

Games usually have two equal periods of playing time. Playing time varies from 30- to 45-minute halves.

A coin toss before the game determines which team will kick off. Play begins with the **kickoff** at the center spot. The players on the team that is not kicking off cannot be in the center circle until one player from the kicking team has kicked the ball. The ball must rotate one full turn before another player can touch it.

The team that does not kick off at the beginning of the game kicks off at the start of the second period. After a team scores a goal, a player from the other team kicks off.

The entire ball must cross the sideline or the goal line for the ball to be out of bounds. When the ball goes out of bounds, it is out of play. If the ball goes out over a sideline, the team that did not send the ball out is awarded a **throw-in.** A player from that team throws the ball back into play. The thrower must be outside of the sideline with both feet on the ground and use both hands to throw the ball directly over his or her head.

If the ball goes out of bounds over the goal line and the team defending the goal last touched it, the opposing team is given a **corner kick.** The corner kick is made from one of the two corner areas on the end of the field where the ball went out of bounds. A player can score on a corner kick alone, but usually the ball is kicked to the area in front of the goal for a teammate to shoot or head into the net.

When the ball goes out over the goal line and the team defending the goal did not touch it last, that team is given a **goal kick.** For a goal kick, the ball is placed in the goal area, usually on the corner. The person taking the goal kick should be able to kick the ball far down the field from a stationary position.

THROW-INS

When a team is awarded a throw-in, the defender or the midfielder playing on the side of the field where the ball went out usually throws.

Standing a short distance from the sideline, the thrower holds the ball with thumbs touching. The player brings the ball up over his or her head while stepping forward. The second step adds momentum, and with the third step, the player throws the ball. Both feet must be on the ground and behind the sideline when the ball is thrown and the ball must go directly over the player's head.

If the player does the throw-in incorrectly, the opposing team is awarded a throw-in at the same place.

YELLOW CARD, RED CARD

If a player is arguing, using foul language, or harassing an official or another player, the referee may show the player a **yellow card**. The yellow card is a caution to the player that any other misconduct will be met with a **red card**. A red card means that the player is expelled from the game. Other actions that can result in a caution or ejection from the game include entering the game without the referee's permission, violent behavior, and wasting time.

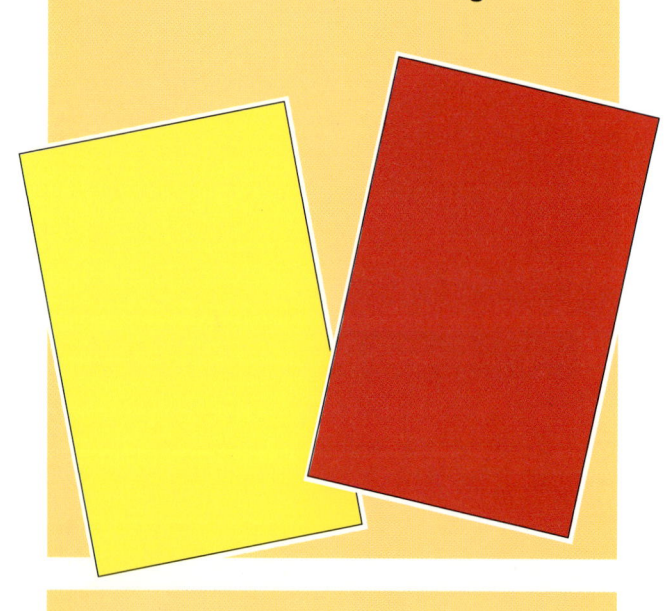

DROP BALL

If the referee has to stop play because of an injury or a foul, the game is restarted with a drop ball. A drop ball takes place at the spot where the ball was last in play.

During a drop ball, one player from each team stands near the referee. The referee blows the whistle, drops the ball between the two players, and play begins.

FOULS

The referee decides when a rule has been broken. **Major violations** include pushing, tripping, holding, and handball. The referee calls handball if a player other than the goalkeeper uses his or her hands to play the ball.

Minor violations of the rules include being **offside.** If a player is closer to the opponent's goal than the ball is, without at least two opposing players between him or her and the goal, offside is called. Offside is not called in corner kick, goal kick, or throw-in situations.

Other minor violations include dangerous play, such as a high kick that could injure another player, and obstruction, which is blocking an opponent rather than going for the ball.

A **direct free kick** is awarded for a major violation. For minor violations, the opposing team gets an **indirect free kick.** Direct and indirect free kicks are taken from the spot where the violation occurred. All players must be at least 10 yards away from the spot where the ball is placed. A direct free kick can score a goal. An indirect free kick can set up a goal, but a second player must touch the ball before it goes into the net.

If a major violation occurs within a team's penalty area, the opponents get a **penalty kick.** The penalty kick is taken from the penalty spot, just 12 yards from the goal line, and only the goalie can defend the goal.

IN ACTION

Let's watch how two teams, the Reds and the Wildcats, put into action the skills already discussed. The Wildcats won the coin toss, so they have the kickoff.

Laura, a forward, kicks the ball forward from the center spot, and Becky makes a long pass out to the wing. Melissa carries the ball down the line until the fullback challenges her and comes up with the ball. The Reds player sends the ball down to the Wildcats' half of the field. The Wildcats hustle back to play defense.

When the Reds' right forward dribbles down toward the Wildcats' goal, Chinda comes up to tackle for the ball. As she does, Marissa—who is playing center fullback—moves over to cover Chinda's territory. After the ball is played out of bounds, Chinda moves back into position as left fullback, and Marissa shifts back.

After about 15 minutes, some of the Wildcats are getting tired. The coach calls for a substitution when the Wildcats have a goal kick. A coach can make substitutions on the field when his or her team has a goal kick or a throw-in. Angelina and Xanara come onto the field to relieve two of the midfielders.

Jenny takes the goal kick, sending the ball downfield to Kacie. Kacie turns and sees an opponent coming at her. Kacie fakes like she is going to

MAKE THAT PASS

The quickest way to move the ball around the field is by passing. Soccer players need to be aware of where their teammates and opponents are. Teams that pass well are successful because the players stay spread out over the field without bunching. If two or three players are in the same spot and one of them gains possession of the ball, the other two won't be in position to receive a pass. And two or three teammates bunched in one place mean many open spaces on the field where the opposing team's players have no competition for the ball. By keeping distance between you and your teammates, you will be better at passing and receiving passes.

the left and dribbles to the right, past the other player! She passes to Xanara. Xanara sees several Reds in front of her, so she passes back to Angelina and sprints downfield to an open spot. Angelina makes a one-touch pass—called a **wall pass**—back to Xanara and Xanara dribbles toward the Reds' goal.

As she approaches the goal line, Xanara makes a long, high kick right in front of the goal. Kacie jumps up and heads the ball toward the goal. She scores!

The Reds take the kickoff. Before the Wildcats' defense gets set up, the Reds pass the ball several times, and take a shot on goal.

Nichole is ready for the high shot and grabs it. She punts the ball back down the field, and Katie yells, "I got it!" She traps the ball with her stomach. A Red is in her way so Katie passes the ball back—a **support pass**—and Emily sends the ball across the field to the left side.

All too soon, the referee blows his whistle for halftime. The Wildcats are ahead by one point. Their coach reminds them to spread out on the field. Many times, two or three players go for the ball, creating a crowded situation and leaving no one open to take a pass. "Make sure you talk to each other and call for the ball," the coach says.

Soon after the second half begins, Angelina gets the ball near the middle of the field. Becky sprints toward the Reds' goal, ready for a pass. Angelina passes the ball to Becky, and the referee blows his whistle. "Offside!" Becky had passed all of the defenders, leaving just the goalie between her and the goal before she got the pass. The Reds get a free kick.

Later, Angelina passes the ball downfield to Becky. This time, a Red defender and the goalie are between Becky and the goal. Becky sprints downfield with the ball and the defender runs up to meet her. Becky fakes a shot. The defender moves to block it and Becky dribbles the ball around her. The Reds goalkeeper comes off the goal line and starts toward Becky. Becky aims and shoots the ball to the lower right corner— another score!

The Reds rush to start the ball in play again. They are two goals behind, and they need to score soon to have a chance to win. The Reds quickly bring the ball toward the Wildcats' goal. Marissa tries to keep the ball out of the penalty area but accidentally kicks it past the goal line. The Reds get a corner kick.

The Wildcats mark up the Reds in front of the goal. The corner kick is a high ball that sails right in front of the goal. A Red forward meets the ball in the air with her foot, volleying it right past Nichole into the goal!

The Wildcats take the kickoff and start play again but soon the referee blows his whistle. The game is over. The Wildcats win! The Reds and Wildcats line up and shake each other's hands.

TOTAL SOCCER

All players attack and all players defend in total soccer. Players fill in at one another's positions on defense and offense. For example, a forward may see that a fullback on her team is challenging an opponent for the ball. Instead of staying upfield, the forward hustles to play defense in case the fullback gets beat. Or, if a fullback has the ball and sees that his best option is to carry the ball upfield instead of passing, he does and a teammate covers his position until he gets back. Teammates who are familiar with one another's skills and playing styles do the best at total soccer.

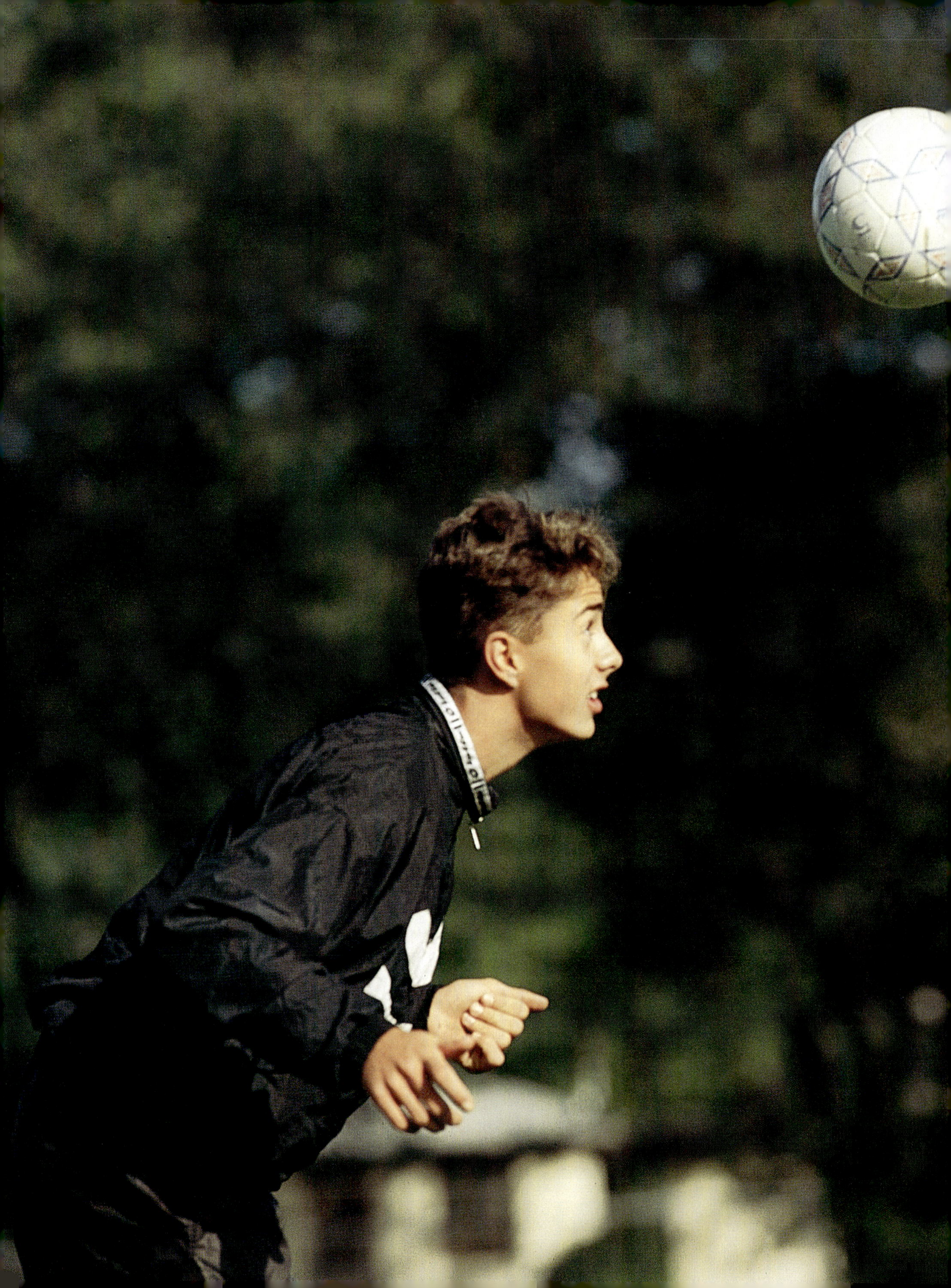

Chapter 4

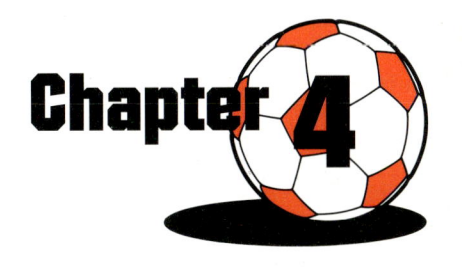

PRACTICE, PRACTICE

Most soccer players practice on the days they don't play games. Each practice session includes some stretching, running, and drills to improve conditioning and skills. Some exercises and drills are illustrated on the following pages.

When you're practicing, first dribble around the soccer field to warm up your body, then stretch all the muscles in your legs, back, arms, and neck. After stretching, do some warm-up exercises.

For example, stand with your feet close together, next to a soccer ball. Then jump over the ball, keeping your feet together, and land on the other side of the ball. Do this 25 times.

On the left, Neil demonstrates the same exercise, but he is jumping over the ball forward and backward. Do this 25 times, too. These exercises help improve coordination and increase leg strength.

Next, do exercises to strengthen your stomach muscles. Get a partner and link ankles with the partner while in sit-up position. Pass a soccer ball back and forth as you do sit-ups. The one with the ball must touch it to the ground behind his or her head before each sit-up.

In another exercise, lie on the ground with a soccer ball between your feet. Lift your feet up six inches off the ground, still holding the ball between them. Then slowly raise your feet even higher, until the ball is directly over your head.

On this page, Erick demonstrates another exercise. First, he throws the ball up, as high and as straight up as possible. Then, he leaps into a somersault, bounds back up, and tries to catch the ball. If he's slow, the ball bounces next to him. But if he finishes the somersault fast enough, he has time to catch the ball in midair.

Sprinting increases speed. Jogging helps build up endurance. One exercise uses both jogging and sprinting. With your teammates, begin jogging around the field in a single line. Then the last one in the line sprints to the front of the line, while everyone else is jogging, and yells for the next person to go. Again, the last one in line sprints to the front and so on.

DRILLS AND SKILLS

Juggling improves ball-handling skills and can be done any time since all you need is a ball. At left, Niels demonstrates juggling. The idea is to keep the ball from touching the ground, using your feet, thighs, head, and any other part of your body except your hands and arms. Keep track of the number of touches you can get in before the ball bounces on the ground.

Dribbling drills are another good way to improve ball-handling skills. For one drill, set up a line of cones a couple of steps apart from one another. Starting at the first cone, dribble forward and weave the ball around each of the cones. When you reach the last cone, quickly turn and weave back through the cones to the starting line.

In another drill, each player gets a ball and stands inside the center circle on the field. When the coach blows the whistle, everyone begins to dribble around the circle, keeping their heads up so that they don't run into each other. The coach calls out different touches that the players must do while continuing to dribble.

When the call is "Inside!" the players make two quick touches with the inside of the foot and then sprint with the ball for a couple of steps before resuming a jogging dribble. When the call is "Outside!" they do the same with the outside of the foot. When the coach yells out "Touch!" the players touch the ball with the bottom of the foot before going on. And when the coach yells "Switch!" they change direction.

After about 10 minutes, the coach changes the drill slightly. Instead of calling a touch to be performed, the coach raises a hand, holding up fingers. The players must all yell out how many fingers the coach is holding up. This drill helps the players get used to dribbling the ball without always looking at it.

On this page, Rachael, Jenny, and Wendy are doing a pass weave. They begin, standing side by side about 10 yards apart. Rachael has the ball in the middle. As they jog forward, Rachael passes the ball to Jenny on the right. Rachael follows her pass and takes Jenny's place as Jenny dribbles to the center. As they all move forward, Jenny passes to Wendy and goes to the left, Wendy takes the ball to the center and passes to Rachael.

In this drill, one defender is in the middle of a circle of passers. Everyone in the circle passes the ball around while the player in the middle tries to block a pass and get the ball. When the player is successful, he or she takes the place of the player whose pass was blocked and that player goes in the middle.

One-on-one play is a good way to practice skills. On this page, Niels and Neil demonstrate a shadowing drill. In this drill, Niels starts with the ball, and Neil follows him closely from behind. Neil does not try to take the ball away from Niels, but he tries to make it difficult for Niels to dribble in the direction he wants to go.

Another way to practice one-on-one play is to set up challenge situations in front of a regular goal.

With the goalkeeper in goal, the other players line up in one of two lines—one at the edge of the goal and one at the top of the goal area. Each player behind the endline has a ball.

The first player in line passes the ball to the first person in the other line. That player must trap the ball and dribble in to try to shoot and score. The player who passed the ball speeds out to play defense against the shooting player.

Playing with fewer players than normal is another way to improve game skills. Six players on a team, three players against one, four players against two, or almost any variation gives players a chance to refine their passing and defending techniques.

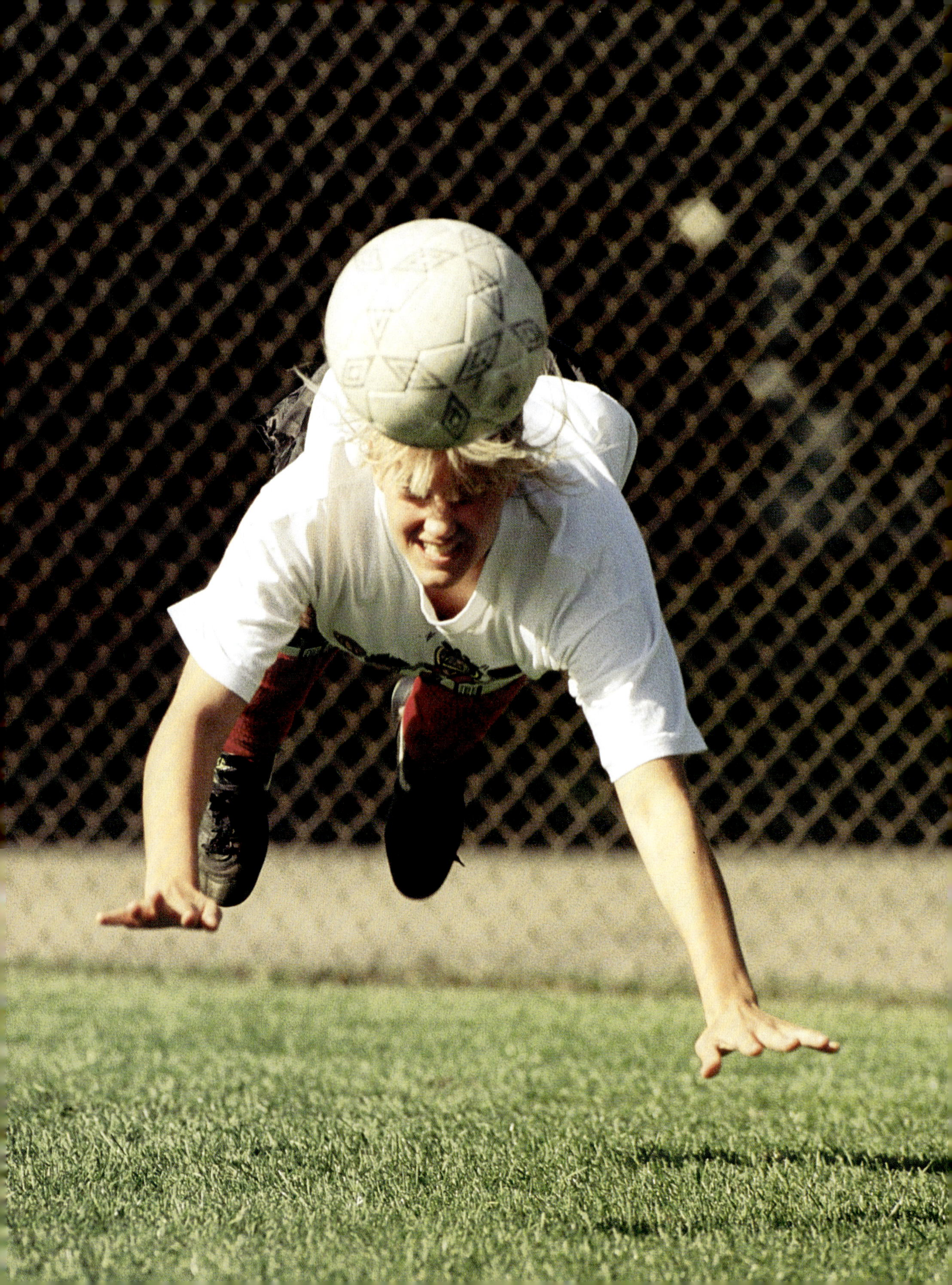

Chapter 5

RAZZLE DAZZLE

Even excellent soccer players practice a lot to develop their skills. With more and more practice, players can perform more skillfully. And the more teammates play together, the better they become at playing together.

The better a player's ball-handling skills, the more he or she will be able to dribble past opponents in a game. For example, a good juggler will be able to use those juggling skills on the field to keep the ball under control while moving toward the goal. Good ball handlers have learned to be creative in their dribbling, using a variety of moves to go in any direction—not just forward. The best players use the width of the field and aren't afraid to dribble out to the sideline or to pass the ball back.

PROFESSIONAL SOCCER

Professional soccer leagues have come and gone in the United States. Once, American players who wanted to earn a living by playing the sport had to travel to Europe and beyond. But those who wish to stay in the United States have an option.

Major League Soccer (MLS) began in 1996 with eight teams. By 1999, the league had grown to 10 teams. Although none of the teams was a money-maker by 1999, television ratings and corporate sponsorships continued to increase.

Following the success of the U.S. women in the 1999 World Cup and the huge fan interest, some sponsors began planning for a women's professional league.

DIVING HEADER

Advanced soccer players have a number of spectacular moves they can use to outsmart and beat opponents as well as to impress fans. One of these moves is the diving header. Diving headers are usually shots on goal, although they may be used to send the ball downfield when under pressure. The advantage of diving to head the ball is that you can get to the ball quickly and powerfully.

Players often learn to do diving headers in a sand pit, so they have a soft place to land while they learn.

On this page, Vas tosses the ball in front of Nate as Nate runs to the goal. Nate dives forward, with his arms out to his sides, and hits the ball with his forehead, keeping his neck firm and his eyes open. Nate lands arms first on the ground to soften the impact.

SLIDING TACKLE

If an opponent breaks away to the goal with the ball, a defender may need to gain possession of the ball quickly. That's when a sliding tackle is effective. Casey demonstrates in the photographs on this page.

Running to make the play, Casey concentrates on the ball. When she is close to the ball, Casey tucks her right leg under and thrusts her left leg out as she slides and contacts the ball. Just before her opponent gets a foot on it, Casey kicks the ball out of her opponent's reach.

SCISSORS KICK

The scissors kick, or bicycle kick, is done by jumping up in a backward somersault motion. In the air, as the kicking foot rises to strike the ball overhead, the nonkicking foot is thrust back and down to provide leverage and to give power to the kick. After kicking the ball, cushion your fall with your arm.

57

THE INDOOR GAME

An indoor soccer field is much smaller—52 yards long and 36 yards wide—than a regulation field. The goals are 12 feet wide and 6½ feet high. Indoor soccer also uses fewer players. Each team has six players, including the goalie, on the field.

Indoor soccer players wear rubber-soled shoes without cleats because indoor playing surfaces are hard.

With less room, players must think and react faster. Big, powerful kicks tend to send the ball out of bounds more often than not. Short, quick, accurate passes and good ball control will help a team win. Shots on goal should be kept low to the ground.

If the ball passes over a sideline and out of bounds, the team that did not last touch it is awarded a **kick in.** A player sets the ball on the sideline at the point where it went out and kicks it back into play.

If the ball goes out of play across the goal line, and the defending team last touched it, the attacking team is awarded a corner kick. One of the players places the ball on the corner, where the sideline and the goal line intersect, and kicks the ball into play. If the attacking team last touched the ball before it crossed the goal line, the defending team is given the ball. The goalie must throw the ball back into play, but the ball cannot cross the center line. In fact, the goalkeeper can never throw, punt, or drop-kick the ball past the halfway line in indoor soccer. If the goalkeeper does, the opposing team is awarded an indirect free kick from the center line.

SOCCER TALK

basic stance: The standing position in which the goalkeeper is on his or her toes, with knees slightly bent and arms out.

center circle: The circle at the center of the field with a radius of 10 yards from the center spot.

center line: The line through the middle of the field that divides the field.

center spot: The spot in the center of the field from which kickoffs are taken.

collect: The technique of receiving a ground or airborne ball and controlling it before putting it in play. Also called trapping.

corner area: The arc around each of the field's four corners. Corner kicks are taken from these areas.

corner kick: A direct free kick taken from the corner area after the ball is played out of bounds past the goal line by the defending team.

crossbar: A bar, 8 yards long, that forms the top boundary of the goal and to which the net is attached.

direct free kick: A free kick that can score a goal without the ball being touched first by another player. A direct free kick is awarded to a team when the opposing team commits a major violation.

diving: A technique used mainly by goalkeepers to make a save.

dribbling: Running while touching the ball with the feet to keep it under control and moving along with the player.

forward: A player position, mainly used for offense. Forwards are usually goal scorers.

fullback: A player position, mainly used for defense. Fullbacks work with the goalkeeper to keep the opposing team from shooting on goal.

goal: The area between the goalposts and the crossbar. A team scores a point when the ball is completely inside the opponent's goal.

goal area: The area immediately around the goal from which goal kicks are taken. The goal area measures 6 yards by 20 yards.

goalkeeper: One of a team's 11 players on the field. As the primary defender of the team's goal, the goalkeeper is the only player who can use his or her hands to play the ball (except for a throw-in).

goal kick: A free kick taken by the team defending the goal after the ball goes out of bounds and was last touched by the opposing team. The goal kick is taken from the goal area.

goalposts: The two bars, both 8 feet tall, that define the boundaries of the goal and to which the crossbar and netting are attached.

heading: A technique used to play the ball by hitting it with the forehead, near the hairline.

heel pass: A pass back to a player in a support position. Instead of turning, the passer stops the ball and hits it back with his or her heel.

indirect free kick: A free kick that cannot score a goal without first being touched by another player. Indirect free kicks are awarded when the opposing team commits a minor violation.

instep: The part of the foot covered by the shoelaces. The instep is used for powerful kicks.

juggling: The technique of keeping the ball in the air by making touches with the feet, thighs, chest, and head.

kick in: In indoor soccer, the method of returning the ball into play after it goes out of bounds over a sideline. A player kicks from the spot where the ball went out of play.

kickoff: The way to begin play at the start of the game, after halftime, and after a goal is scored. The ball is played from the center spot and must rotate one full turn before it is touched by another player. During a kickoff, opposing players must stay outside of the center circle.

major violation: A foul for which the opposing team is awarded a direct free kick.

marking: The technique of defending an opponent in which a player stays close to the opponent, guarding against an attack by him or her.

midfielder: A position on the field between the forwards and the fullbacks. Midfielders must play both offense and defense.

minor violation: A foul for which the opposing team is awarded an indirect free kick.

offside: A player is offside if he or she is on the opponents' half of the field with only one opponent between the player and the goal when the ball is played.

one-touch pass: A technique used to receive the ball and pass it on with only one touch.

passing: Playing the ball to a teammate by kicking or heading it.

penalty arc: The arc connected to the penalty area. Players must stand outside of this arc during a penalty kick.

penalty area: The large area marked in front of each goal, which surrounds the goal area. The goalkeeper may use his or her hands to play the ball only within this area. If a major violation is committed within the penalty area by the defending team, the opposing team is awarded a penalty kick.

penalty kick: A direct free kick taken after a major violation is committed by the opponents in their own penalty area. The penalty kick is taken from the penalty spot.

penalty spot: The spot from which penalty kicks are taken. The penalty spot is located 12 yards in front of the center of the goal.

punts: One of the ways a goalkeeper may put the ball into play after making a save. The goalie holds the ball out in front and makes an aerial kick with his or her laces.

red card: The referee's signal to inform a player that he or she is expelled from the game.

shooting: An attempt to score a goal by kicking, heading, or otherwise touching the ball to send it toward the goal.

shot on goal: An attempt to score a goal that requires the goalkeeper to stop the ball for a save.

support pass: A pass to a teammate positioned behind the passer.

tackling: A defensive technique used to take the ball from an opponent.

throw-in: The method of returning the ball into play after it has been played out of bounds over the sideline by an opponent.

trapping: Coming into possession of the ball by collecting and controlling it.

volley pass: A one-touch pass made in the air.

wall pass: A one-touch pass made to the player from whom the ball was received.

wing: A player in the outside forward position.

yellow card: A referee's warning signal to a player to inform him or her that another misconduct will result in being expelled from the game.

FURTHER READING

Bauer, Gerhard. *Soccer Techniques, Tactics and Teamwork*. New York, New York: Sterling Publishing Co., Inc., 1993.

Blatter, Joseph S. *Soccer Rules Explained*. New York, New York: The Lyons Press, 1998.

Caligiuri, Paul. *High-Performance Soccer: Techniques and Tactics for Advanced Play*. Champaign, Illinois: Human Kinetics Publishers, 1996.

Glanville, Brian. *The Story of the World Cup*. London, England: Faber & Faber, 1997.

Luxbacher, Joseph A. *Soccer Practice Games*. Champaign, Illinois: Human Kinetics Publishers, 1994.

Murray, Bill. *The World's Game: A History of Soccer*. Champaign, Illinois: University of Illinois Press, 1998.

Phillips, Lincoln. *Soccer Goalkeeping: The Last Line of Defense, the First Line of Attack*. Indianapolis, Indiana: Masters Press, 1996.

Savage, Jeff. *Julie Foudy*. Minneapolis, Minnesota: Lerner Publishing Group, 1999.

Strachan, Gordon. *Getting Started in Soccer*. New York, New York: Sterling Publishing Co., Inc., 1994.

FOR MORE INFORMATION

American Youth Soccer Organization (AYSO)
2501 South Isis Avenue
Hawthorne, CA 90250
www.soccer.org

Federation Internationale de Football Association (FIFA)
P. O. Box 85
8030 Zurich, Switzerland
www.fifa.com

U. S. Soccer Federation (USSF)
Olympic Village
1750 East Boulder Street
Colorado Springs, CO 80909
www.us-soccer.com

U. S. Youth Soccer Association (USYSA)
2050 North Plano
Suite 100
Richardson, TX 75082
www.usysa.org

INDEX

balls, 12
center circle, 11
center line, 11
center spot, 11
cleats, 12, 58
collecting, 26–27
conditioning, 43–46
corner areas, 11
corner kick, 35, 41
crossbar, 11

defense 23–24, 37
diving, 29–30
diving header, 54
dribbling, 13–14, 46–47
drop ball, 36

fake, 14
Federation Internationale de Football Association (FIFA), 9
football, 8
forwards, 33
free kick, 36
fullbacks, 33

goal, 11
goal area, 11
goalkeeper, 12, 25
goalkeeping, 25–31
goal kick, 35
goalposts, 11

header, 22, 38

indoor soccer, 58

juggling, 46

kickoff, 34

London Football Association, 8

major violations, 36
marking, 23
Meola, Tony, 27
midfielders, 32, 33–34
minor violations, 36

offside, 36, 39

passing, 15–17, 37, 48–49; heel, 16; one-touch, 16; volley, 17
pass weave, 48
penalty arcs, 11

penalty area, 11
penalty kick, 36
penalty spot, 11
positioning, 25
professional soccer, 53
punts, 31

red card, 36
Romans, 8
rugby, 8
rules, 34–35

scissors kick, 56–57
shoes, 12, 58
shooting, 20
sliding tackle, 55
soccer field, 11

stretching, 43
support pass, 38

tackling, 23–24
throw-in, 35
total soccer, 41
trapping, 18–19

United States Soccer Federation (USSF), 9

wall pass, 38
wings, 33
World Cup, 9

yellow card, 36